COME SHARE THE COOKIES

Laughing, Loving, and Praying Without Ceasing

by

Diane Thompson

Gotham Books

30 N Gould St.
Ste. 20820, Sheridan, WY 82801
https://gothambooksinc.com/

Phone: 1 (307) 464-7800

© 2024 *Diane Thompson*. All rights reserved.

No part of this book may be reproduced, stored in a retrieval system, or transmitted by any means without the written permission of the author.

Published by Gotham Books (May 4, 2024)

ISBN: 979-8-88775-758-2 (P)
ISBN: 979-8-88775-759-9 (E)

Because of the dynamic nature of the Internet, any web addresses or links contained in this book may have changed since publication and may no longer be valid.

The views expressed in this work are solely those of the author and do not necessarily reflect the views of the publisher, and the publisher hereby disclaims any responsibility for them.

CONTENTS

Dedicated to vii
1 Let's Share the Cookies 1
2 Twinkle or Reflection 4
3 Huh? 6
4 I Have the Answer 8
5 He's Still Counting 11
6 Pass It On 13
7 The Wake-up Call 16
8 Comfy 19
9 The Chicken Was Delicious 22
10 The Twins 25
11 To Degree or Not To Degree? 28
12 Blueprints 31
13 Questions? Questions? Questions? 34
14 1413 Euca…. Oak 37
15 A Firm Foundation 39
16 If the Shoe Fits! 41
17 Two Ears To Hear 43
18 "Pig!" 45
19 Warnings 48
20 A Sheep in Cat's Clothing 50
21 Christian Incognito 53

22 The Phone Call 55

23 God Made Me Woman 58

24 Pressure Escapes 60

25 Soul Weary 62

26 The Enabler 65

27 Selective Weakness 67

28 Disabling Expectations 70

29 Black, White and Gray 73

30 A Name Above All Names 76

31 That One Black Spot 79

32 The Unwrapped Gift 81

33 Good Grief 83

Dedicated to

Tim, Ronnie; Beth, Bryan; Steve, Kim and to those precious children who call me Mams, Nana and Grand mommy.

I hope you enjoy reading this book as much as I enjoyed writing it. I wanted each of you to know the very essence of who Dad and I were and some of what we cherished.

I used to say our marriage was not perfect. Maybe that is God's plan for all our marriages but our love came pretty close to perfect. I never doubted Gil's love for me and I am confident that he knew how much I loved him and I know that our love for God is what made it the kind that would last a lifetime.

I know each of you will have years that you would rather not look back on, except to thank God that you made it through them and you grew in your understanding of each other just as we did.

I wish I could have taped some of the "goodnight, head on the pillow talk" so you could have known how much we enjoy each one of you and how proud we are of what each one of you has become. I don't mean your professions. I see kindness, gentleness, a care for others and a desire to seek God. I see determination, pride, and resourcefulness. I see work ethics and disciplines that can't be matched and then there is the creativity and humor that make life just a little more enjoyable.

I think it is important for you to know that when I look back, I could dwell on some significant hurts and misunderstandings but I keep seeing a beautiful smile and I hear laughter and I feel a strong sense of having been loved. I miss him terribly. He gave us so much more than what this world values as an inheritance.

I continually pray that God blesses each one of you along with all the grandchildren. I think that it is important for you to know that your name is poured out to God every single day.

It goes without saying…. I love you so much…. Mom.

Victor Hugo once said "There is one thing stronger than all the armies in the world, and that is an idea whose time has come."

For 55 years, it had not even dawned on me that I was a writer. My first clue should have been when I realized that there absolutely wasn't anything about which I didn't have an opinion. For five years I published a weekly newsletter for my church. No one else seemed to want to do it, and it was something that I loved doing.

The fourteen years that I worked as an insurance agent should also have given me a nudge. I often gave group presentations that included stories about so many of my life experiences. Many clients encouraged me to write them down and share them with others. But it took a life-changing crisis that made me take a look within and find why God had placed me here.

I have written a collection of insights that I gained during the first half of my life. Each chapter begins with a joke, a thought or a scripture that I believe God laid on my heart. The body of each chapter consists of a related experience, insight or lesson that I gained. And each chapter is completed with a prayer.

I have noticed how people are enjoying inspirational books that are also a "quick" read such as mine. I submitted Chapter Five to the Indianapolis Star and it was published in the Faith and Values section of that newspaper. I think that one sign that a book could be good is when the reader wants more. Each person who has read these chapters did exactly that and asked if they can pass on to others what they have enjoyed or gained from my book.

I would like to thank you in advance for taking the time to read some of what I believe God has shown me in my life. Come Share The Cookies.

Lord, bless this reader,

Amen.

1
Let's Share the Cookies

An old man lay in his upstairs bedroom dying. Suddenly the aroma of fresh-baked chocolate chip cookies right out of the oven reached him. They smelled sooo good that he gathered enough energy to pull himself out of bed. Through his pain, he dragged himself down the stairs and into the kitchen. As he arrived at the table and reached for some cookies, his wife smacked his hands and scolded "Stop that, those are for your funeral."

OK! So you have heard this joke over and over, but isn't it funny? Would I do that? NEVER! Have I done anything even remotely so? Well, probably. My first thought, among many, is about my oldest son, Tim, and my husband, Gil. Tim has always been an entrepreneur—from mowing lawns and snow removal jobs as a teenager up to advertising the business he and his wife have begun. I sit back and see how his wife fosters this trait in him and "allows" him to explore different outlets for his talents. Though they both know that some of their ventures will not succeed, I watch with pride as they encourage each other, both investing time and energy in the research and development of each new undertaking.

But when I reflect on the path that Gil and I have taken, I hear the echoes of "There just is not enough money to pay the bills." "That job does not pay enough; you could make so much more." "I am the only one making a living here!" I think of all the people I have encouraged. The people I have trained and the skills that I have passed on to others, and yet my own family could have been "dying" and needing my "cookies"! So I am asking you, the reader, to stick with me through this adventure. I hope to share some of the humor, wisdom and life experiences of my family and friends. I hope you can grasp some of the aroma as I share just a morsel of what God is teaching me as He molds me into the final "Batch of Cookies" that He wants me to share with all of you.

Lord, I need help breaking the mold that I have made for myself and each of my family members. May I never take them for granted or forget how precious and special each one is. Bless the reader and their family. Maybe through sharing my struggles and growth, they can see themselves or someone in their family. Also, Lord, please be patient with this reader and forgiving of my humor and satire. I just can't help it!

So, today, I will start by passing out all the cookies I have been saving.

2

Twinkle or Reflection

You know you are getting more mature when the twinkle in your eye is merely a reflection from the sun on your bifocals.

When you were young, did you ever wonder what "love" would look like as you grew older? Before Gil came and picked me up for our first date he had a dozen yellow roses delivered to my front door. How could one not have a great evening after that? If we enjoyed a song while we were out on a date, he would later buy me the record to remember the date by. He made the plans for most of the dates, and he always held the door for me. Looking back, I think maybe those kinds of courtesies and respect were some of the best things that I enjoyed in the 60s.

Gil may now wear trifocals, but I am sure there are still times the glint can get past those three lines. We are on our 33rd year now. Some would call us mere babes, others could not even comprehend a union that long. I sometimes believe Gil is better at this "love thing" than I am. I really always tried to be a helpmate, but more often than not I might have been the mate needing help.

If you were to ask me about the problems that we had faced in our marriage, I would be able to go into great length about how we handled each one and maybe even have a little emotion still attached. Ask Gil. He would tell you that any problems that may have arisen were only stepping stones that drew us closer. His stones may not have been as sharp as mine! But, sure enough, I will see that twinkle as he tells our story. Can I tell you to stick with it? It will not always be easy, and one of you may do more changing than the other. There will be times when you are right. But is that the objective?

There will be times when you could pick out 50 major flaws in your partner. But what is the point? If I have learned nothing else, it is that I can either dwell on the things that need changing or I can look for and encourage all the positive and good things about the man I have become one with. Because, you see, I can't buy that twinkle, nor can I teach someone to have it. I can't explain what "it" is. I only know that my life blossoms when I see that reflection in my husband's eyes.

You have made it so phenomenal, God! I am me, but I am also one with another. How can I say "Thank You"? You have even deemed that we come together in spirit as we worship You. Because You are our foundation, I know what we have will not crumble, but will stand on Your solid rock. I am grateful for each day we share this life together.

3

Huh?

While at the doctor's office for his annual physical, an elderly gentleman expressed his concern about his wife's hearing. The doctor asked, "How bad is it? How far away do you have to be before she can't hear conversation?" He recommended that the husband go home and talk to her at different distances and see how close he had to be in order to be heard. He went home, and as he entered the door he yelled "Honey, I am home. What is for dinner?" No response. Then he went into the living room, "Honey, I am home. What is for dinner?" Again, no response. Finally he went into the kitchen where his wife stood, hands on hips with a look of scorn. He stated that three times he had called to her and she had not answered. To which she replied "AND FOR THE FOURTH TIME—CHICKEN!"

Have you not been there? Knowing full well what you believe to be true, and concerned that others just don't seem to "get it"? You are so confident that it is a black-and-white situation, then through time, experience, or even new information, a "dogma" changes. (Wait, is that an oxymoron?) I remember so vividly an example when I was a young stay-at-home mother.

Money was tight, and I prided myself on my frugality. I sewed and gave everyone handmade Christmas gifts. Garage sales provided the money for any vacations we took. But, where I tried my hardest was grocery shopping. I cut coupons, cooked from scratch, and every newspaper ad was devoured. That brings me to "my dogma" —Chef's Delight Cheese. At that time, it cost 69 cents for a block of cheese, and my family loves cheese. I saw the Velveeta on the shelf, but I knew it was in no way better than my cheese and it cost $1.19. Almost double! How could people be so wasteful? They must not be good stewards of their money. How many times did I want to stop those women and point out what a value they were passing up? One day my store had a special, and I had a coupon. What was the worst that could happen? We tried the Velveeta. I then realized what I had missed all those years. Some things cannot be measured by money! My passion changed immediately. I try to remember this after all these years. As new cultural and intergenerational ideas and teachings barge into my life, I tend to take one side immediately and with passion. Then I have to remind myself to back off and weigh each side and put things into perspective.

Lord, open my heart and my mind. Help me to understand that You have given each of us different needs and talents. It is not the willingness to change that causes me problems. It is more like understanding what should be changed. Lead me.

4

I Have the Answer

An older gentleman was seated next to a young blond woman on an eight-hour airplane trip. To pass the time, the gentleman told the woman that she could ask him any question, and if he could not answer it, he would pay her $5.00. Then he would ask her a question, and if she did not know the answer, she would pay him $5.00. She was tired and shook her head as she curled up with a book. So he raised the ante and said he would pay her $50.00 if she asked him a question he could not answer, and he would still receive $5.00 if she could not answer his questions. To get him off her back, she asked, "What goes up the stairs with four legs and comes down the stairs with three legs?" For several hours he searched through his computer encyclopedia. He even used his cell phone and called the Library of Congress. He called several professors he knew and none of them knew the answer. Finally, he turned to her as she slumbered and shook her, saying that he gave up. Handing her the $50.00, he asked for the answer. She took the $50.00 and handed him back the $5.00, stating that she did not know either.

I have been told that not everyone enjoys my jokes as much as I do. I have read this joke over and over and still appreciate the scene. It might be because it reminds me of myself and many members of my family. We share such a passion for learning that we forget that some people just want to relax. We recently have set up two websites for all our family members to "chat" and share news. In many ways, it has been a blessing and has drawn some of the younger cousins closer together who have moved far away. It has been a forum where each person can share a thought, feeling, or idea without interruption. Can you not separate your family into the two categories that the gentleman and the blond lady could represent? One would be seeking the challenge, the other taking a time out. One proud of the knowledge he has gained, and the other content with his present state of mind. The best comes at the last. How many times do you think you have your act together? You are ready for the challenge. You might even shake your fist at Satan's face because you are on top of the world. Daily devotions, tithe paid, great sermon Sunday, even shared the gospel this week.

Then, out of the blue, at a moment's notice, a crisis arises and questions begin flowing. "Why, God?" "What next?" "Are You there?" There are times I want God to give me all the answers. I sometimes forget that my walk is a walk of faith." I believe. Help me unbelieve." This is my prayer.

Lord, when I feel I need an answer, help me to know it is only You I need. You are Omnipotent. You will have the final say. I am learning to let go of needing to always understand.

5

He's Still Counting

There are three kinds of people: those who can count and those who can't.

That takes me back to when things just didn't add up for me. I remember when our daughter Elizabeth was born. We had our girl. We were so excited when we had her dedicated at our home church. Even when we visited the church my husband had come from, they insisted that they get to dedicate her also. Many times we have fondly jested that she was twice blessed. What a joy she has been! Today she is a beautiful woman who possesses empathy for people who are oppressed, neglected or in need, emotionally, physically or spiritually. She seems to be able to reach the core problem of each need. This trait was acquired by a couple of life-changing events. You know what I mean. You probably have had many yourselves, Financial ruin, accidents, surprise pregnancy, maybe even a death…. the list goes on. Bethy (who knows when we started calling her that?) was having one of her best years at Ball State. She was working her way through school and it wasn't always easy making the best grades with few hours to study, but this semester was going to be one of her best. It was time for finals and she was prepared. But while she was walking home one evening, she was attacked and wound up in the hospital. The school gave permission to go back and finish finals later, but at the time she could not imagine going back. She lost her credits, not to mention her sense of safety and well-being. As a mother, I know of nothing that can hurt a heart more than seeing a child hurt, and then witnessing the struggles that result from the scars. But even deeper were the questions thrown at God. We dedicated her! We raised her with Christian principles. Where was the hedge of protection? How could such a sin defile a child we had dedicated? It hurt too much! How could I trust again, knowing I had three children who could be so vulnerable? For a period of time, I must admit that my faith and trust were weak. Answers do not always come quickly. Two years later, she shared with us some growth that she had gained by the experience, how she was able to relate to so many others in the same circumstances. I had mentally used all the old clichés: "All things work together for good... He won't give you more than you can handle..." I remember crying uncontrollably when I heard her words. I marveled at how she could see the good when I saw only pain and exposure. It was then when God's words were no longer clichés. If He could bear such pain for my family, then I can also handle what he needs for His family.

Lord, it is all yours! I know You can count. It may not always add up the way I think it should, but I know You make no mistakes. All that I foolishly think is mine, I give to You.

6

Pass It On

Bumper sticker on large luxury RV: We're spending our children's inheritance.

When I first saw this, I believed it meant money, but the more I put in the light of God's teachings, I became overwhelmed with the ramifications. I have so much to leave to my children and grandchildren. It started the moment they were born.

The first thing I value is our faith and walk with God. It has not been perfect and I know our children remember every mistake we ever made. Even the traditions we pass on are important. Sunday mornings at our home, Gil would be the first up and he would start singing. Every one of our kids was still in a comatose state. They hated getting up, especially when Dad was enjoying his best day and was in such a good mood. Meeting with our brothers and sisters in Christ has always been our refuge and our strength. If they receive nothing more for their inheritance than knowing that their mother and father loved God and wanted only to draw them closer to Him each day, then that would be enough.

Another value we want to pass down is the importance of giving time and individual attention to our children. I look around at families who are so busy making a living and trying to accumulate "stuff" and letting their children get all the leftovers. It is not easy. Even in the church, there is a tendency to get too busy. I even remember my mother expressing concern about all the ballgames, school plays and music programs. (Do we ever stop mothering?) It was exhausting but enjoyable to see each child develop. Our children knew their interests were always important to us. Much of our time was spent in playing family games. Still is! I loved watching the interaction and strategy, and the way each learned to communicate needs and frustrations. I love competition, so we probably could have done better teaching that winning isn't as important as "how we played the game." I cannot stop without mentioning our sense of humor. I don't know how humorless families make it. (They may wonder about us also!) I remember a problem which I thought I could handle no more. I had been sharing it for weeks with my best friend, Bobbie, to no avail. Neither of us could come up with a solution. I hurt so much that all it took was for anyone to ask me how I was doing for me to break into tears. This particular Sunday was the worst. After church, we went to our favorite restaurant with friends.

During a conversation, I had to rush to the restroom, for if I had stayed, everyone would know that I was going to cry. Bobbie followed me. As I was sobbing and sharing, I looked up to see her taking paper towels and wiping all the sinks and faucets clean (we used to clean houses together). This may not be funny to you, but it threw the two of us into a state of hysteria. I am grateful that all of our children can relish this humor. I wish we could give them more financially. But God knows best. Each one has achieved their own financial independence. They have gained pride and independence through hard work and discipline. It has given them understanding and compassion when they see others struggle financially, and I know it has given them the desire to share and encourage others.

Lord, help me to examine the significance of what I am leaving to my family. I want to pass on to them memories and values that they will kept long after I am gone.

7

The Wake-up Call

Jimmy got a parrot for Christmas. The parrot had a bad attitude and worse vocabulary. Every other word was an expletive. Jimmy tried to change the bird's attitude by constantly saying polite words, playing soft music, anything he could think of. Nothing worked. He yelled at the bird and the bird only got worse. He shook the bird and the bird only got madder. Finally, Jimmy put the parrot in the freezer. For a few moments he heard the bird swearing and squawking. Suddenly, there was absolute quiet. Jimmy opened the freezer door. The parrot calmly stepped out onto Jimmy's extended arm and said: "I am sorry that I offended you with my language and my actions, and I ask your forgiveness. I will change my behavior." Jimmy was astounded at the changes in the bird's attitude and was about to ask what had changed him, when the parrot said: "May I ask what the chicken did?"

There is an old saying: "You're an idiot if you do the same thing over and over and expect to have different results." I have looked in the mirror and I swear I don't know who that fat, old woman is who keeps following me! I have asked myself what it would take to change. Would I change my eating habits on my own—NO! Would I take time out of my busy day and exercise routinely—NO! Each of us has destructive habits that we know we should change, but we seem to lack the motivation for that change. Mine has come through a physical challenge. When I was an insurance agent, I loved being out and meeting and talking to people, but my days could get very long and I basically lived on the road. So eating fast food was my norm. I was too exhausted when I got home to go and exercise. Then, gradually things began to change for me. I couldn't concentrate, and pressures seemed to turn me into an emotional basket case. Those signs should have been enough, but I continued in the same patterns. There was even one day on a flight to Florida, where my husband was taking me to "get away" for a week. I sat by a beautiful, elegant older lady. She told me this was her first flight since her stroke six months earlier. She was embarrassed about her speech, and her daughter was going to pick her up at the airport because she easily became disoriented. For one hour she told me her story. Her life had paralleled mine so closely. I knew God had sent her there as a wake-up call. Did I listen? No. Where do we get off thinking what we do is so important in life? That only we can do the job before us? Sometimes we have talents in certain areas and do such a great job to the point that we are almost indispensable. But it may not be what God wants us to do. Every day for six months following that encounter, I could not get the woman out of my mind. Then God—I know He gets blamed for things that we sometimes cause—got my attention.

I continually break out with an awful rash covering my body. It has taken over a year now, and we still do not have a diagnosis. I sometimes grin when I think, "I didn't change right away so why should my condition change right away?" But let me tell you what happened. I LISTENED. I no longer sell insurance. I work out a minimum of 1 hour per day. I watch what I eat. But best of all, I write. Why did I take so long to get to where God really wanted me? What are your excuses? Money? Prestige? Security? Undisciplined? The list goes on and on.

Lord, I want to listen, but I am so used to doing it my way. I have listened to all the motivational tapes. I have seen how the world defines success. Help me to remember that Your ways are not man's ways and that You have a better plan for each of us.

8

Comfy

There once was a man who had a wife who was so neat that she would put a newspaper under her cuckoo clock.

Let me straighten things out right now! I have never been accused of being too neat. But I have found that I work better and can relax more when things are in order. Have you been in homes where you took your shoes off as you entered and you were afraid to even put a glass down? Everything sparkled.

I wonder how comfortable those homes are to the ones who live there. Does anyone relax? Who is doing all the work? A friend came to visit once, and she gave me one of the best compliments of my life. She walked in the door and said that it felt so comfy. Like a great big teddy bear whose arms were just hugging her every time she walked in.

We started out in a two-bedroom mobile home, 12 x 52. We were there until our second child was three years old. So you can imagine how tiny it had become. We had a brown, oval, braided rug that filled the whole front room. When we moved to our next home, it fit perfectly in the HALLWAY. Gil and I took the smallest bedroom. Three sides of the bed rested against the walls. In the children's room we had a trundle bed that we pulled out at night and put away during the day so the kids would have a place to play. At that time, we were also volunteer youth leaders at our church. We never thought twice about opening our home to the teens. The summers would get so hot, I remember one time that we opened all the doors and windows and the heat melted all the cheese on the crackers we were serving. As you can see, we weren't serving the most elegant of meals either! I knew those teenagers were there because we loved them, not because of the food or shelter. Many times, they would bring their dates just to see if we approved. Plus, they knew we would all have fun. Gil even had an overnighter with the boys where they played football in the living room. I can't even imagine what they used for goal posts! They didn't tell me about it for a couple of months. That youth group grew from eight to over seventy within a year and a half. Today, I think of Mary and Martha. Do I give more time to keeping order in my life and home than worshipping and serving the Lord? It has to be done—the wash, the meals, the cleaning, and even the maintenance of the home, but at what expense? I have a larger home now, and all three of my children are gone. My meals are a lot more lavish. But when was the last time I entertained strangers? You know who I mean. The new couple at church, the missionaries who have left their families back home. The new widow in our church. The new couple down the street who just moved in. I know if I keep thinking, the Lord will to start to prod me. My youngest son, Steve, kindly confronted me the other night. He reminded me of all the things we "used" to do but inquired about "what are we doing now?" He and his wife are getting so involved in the workings and outreach of the church. I let him know how proud I was of them and how it was time for the younger people to carry the load. Do you think he bought that excuse?

Lord, you know I am tired. I pretend that there are plenty of others who can do Your work. I even think that it would be good for them. I am grateful for the material blessings that You have given us. Help me to open my home and my heart to the needs of those around me. Help me to see where I am most needed and give me the energy, and the desire to be Your vessel.

9

The Chicken Was Delicious

There were three sons who had reached a measure of success in their lives and decided to get their elderly mother a Christmas gift. The first built his mother an expensive house. The second bought his mother an expensive car. The third knew how much his mother loved reading the Bible, so he found a parrot that had been trained for years to recite the Bible. All she had to do was tell it the chapter and verse, and he would repeat it. After the mother received her three presents, she sent each a letter. The first son she thanked, but stated the house was too big. She lived in only two rooms, but had to clean it all. The second son she thanked, but stated that she was too old to drive, and that she stayed home most of the time. But the third son she wrote: Thank you for the good sense to know what I like. The chicken was delicious.

Another Christmas season is just now coming to an end. Christmas is my favorite time of year. I really try to keep things in balance and not put the true meaning on a back burner.

We have a young family next door who put so much of themselves in the celebration of Christmas. He starts the week after Thanksgiving by coming over and putting our lights on our house—now that is above and beyond.

The week before Christmas, she takes boxes of homemade goodies to each neighbor, all 22 homes. The letter that she encloses is so beautiful. She reminds us of God's greatest gift, and this year the letter invited everyone over for the singing of Christmas carols. Even those who could only make a "Joyful Noise" were invited. One year, they even had a birth announcement in their yard on Christmas day.

It stated that it was a boy, and they should call him Jesus. The neighbors on the other side are also Christians, but do not participate in any celebration of Christmas. From what they have studied, they believe it to have Pagan origins. They even have the pamphlets to explain how "off track" Christians are in the way we celebrate. I do understand their concerns. I sometimes imagine God looking down at each of us and thinking, "They don't get it!" That wasn't the way it was supposed to be. On the other hand, there was probably a reason Jesus could not convince the Pharisees. I don't know if we should be more concerned with the letter of the law or just express God's love in any and every way we can. Our daughter, Beth, has also been concerned that Christmas has gotten out of hand, so she started her own tradition last year. She challenged all of us to celebrate in a non-material way.

She wrote a different poem to each of us about our individual personalities and had them framed. They were so precious. I still read mine over and over. She also gave Gil and me dance lessons. Now you have to understand—neither of us has ever danced, been to a dance, or even went for a walk and kept the same pace. It took six months before we gathered the courage to take the lessons. We experienced so much during those lessons. Our instructor said it was rare to have women doing the reverse leading. I am learning to follow, and Gil is enjoying a bit too much this "take charge" role. We could hardly wipe the smiles off our faces after each lesson. I cannot even tell you how exhausting dancing is. Now I know the reason dancers are so tiny. I have told Beth that her gift is renewed every time I hear music. This year she has enrolled me at our local college for writing and publishing courses. I can hardly wait. She gave Gil computer lessons. I do know the reason for the season, Lord.

You have given me so many people to love, and I truly enjoy finding those special things to give each one, but help me to celebrate Your birth in the most holy of ways. Keep me on track. Help me to see those who have no one to love and care for all year long. Let me see those I could help who have unmet needs. Forgive any misguided expression of Your birth.

10

The Twins

There is a guy who received free tickets to the Super Bowl. Unfortunately, when he arrives at the stadium he is closer to the Goodyear Blimp than to the field. About halfway through the first quarter he notices an empty seat right on the 50-yard line, just a couple of rows up. He takes a chance and works his way down to the empty seat. As he sits down, he asked the gentleman sitting next to him: "Excuse me, is anyone sitting here?" The man says "No." Now excited, he asks the man next to him "Who in his right mind would have a seat like this at the Super Bowl and not use it?" The man replies: "Well, actually, the seat belongs to me. I used to come with my wife but she passed away. This is the first Super Bowl we haven't been together since we got married 40 years ago." "That's sad," said the man, "but still, couldn't you find someone to take the seat? A relative or close friend?" "No," the man replies, "they're still at the funeral."

Moderation! I know I have read that word somewhere in the scriptures. Look around society. Do you see much of it? How about the church? Or the home? Or our own personal lives? I would love to take off running with how sports have consumed our lives. How many TV channels are dedicated to just that one subject? How many players are spokespersons for each product we buy?

Don't get me started on the heroes they have become for our children. Do we really want our children growing up to live lives like the majority of our sports figures? I can't get that Olympic runner off my mind who would not run for the gold because the finals were run on a Sunday. But I won't go there. The beam in my own eye is too big. I also wonder how I became so compulsive. Several years ago, I got into apples. Yep. They were on my wallpaper, on the rugs, on my kitchen table. It was almost like "Where's Waldo?" Each picture on the wall had some token of an apple. Every gift-giving occasion added to my apple collection. It was beautiful when it began, but what happened? When did that need for apples disappear? Today, I can hardly bring myself to eat an apple. Three months ago, I began my workout compulsion. If I missed a day, I was a mess. I truly loved every second. I could hardly wait to get there. I knew it made me feel and look better. Christmas and New Years slowed me down and now I have to force myself each day to go back. I believe moderation has a twin called discipline, and they go hand in hand. This New Year I am trying to examine how I perceive the way I live my life.

I realize that I have always perceived discipline as a negative. The more I examine the very nature of discipline, I realize how necessary and beautiful it is. I have dealt too much with the denial part, versus the process of becoming. I know you won't get to know me unless I discipline myself to sit down and write this book and I want you to know me! I know I won't be size 10 unless I exercise and I want to be a size 10. I know I won't learn anything God wants me to be without reading His Word, and I want to be what God wants me to be. This just doesn't stop, does it? Oops! Another compulsion.

I love the drive you have given me, Lord, but too many times, I let it get out of hand. Let me see that the process of becoming is as important as what I will become. That moderation and discipline are my friends. For this I will give a big AMEN.

11

To Degree or Not To Degree?

(IS THAT THE QUESTION?)

The graduate with a science degree asks, "Why does it work?" The graduate with an engineering degree asks, "How does it work?" The graduate with an accounting degree asks, "How much will it cost?" The graduate with an arts degree asks, "Do you want fries with that?"

What does that make the person without *any* degree ask? Does education only come through the discipline of formal training or can there be as great an education in other paths that we pursue? For whatever sacrifices have been made to either obtain a degree or to not obtain a degree, the most important issue at hand is that a person should never stop learning. I prefer to learn by choice, but many times knowledge races through the door by surprise. I met a stranger in a group of people the other day. I was expressing the wish for something I wanted to happen, but that I didn't believe would happen. With a startled look and eyes that pierced like a bullet, she let me know that she could not understand anyone being so negative. She let me know that she would never think that way. I have since forgotten the issue, but not the woman and her admonition. It has taken me into my 50s to distinguish good teaching from bad.

Do I learn by punishment, discipline or "time outs"? I had never heard of the phrase "time out" when my children were little, and now there's a chair just for that occasion. I do wish they would make them bigger. I sure could use some "time outs." I have observed families who taught by using positive reinforcement and encouraged their children to be all that they could be. My parents were just striving to make a living, put food on the table, and make sure we loved the Lord. Most of their teaching was a by-product of circumstances and necessities. But somehow each of us received from them a desire to learn. I have discarded some of my parents' "methods" of teaching, and have realized that some things that were right for them are just not right for me. No, I do not have to do the wash every Monday. Then iron on Tuesday. (Isn't permanent press wonderful!) As my children are filtering through what we have taught them, I hope they at least keep the "good stuff." I think that the most I can hope for in my children is that they know that I didn't do everything the way they would have done it but I did what I knew to do and believed to be right. And I am still learning.

We have been taught so much in the raising of our children, Lord. How else would I know to just sit and "reflect" on what I just did? You ask us to come as children. Sometimes

I make it too hard. I am taking Your hand now, please be patient — I sometimes have a hard time keeping up.

12

Blueprints

Commit your work to the Lord, then it will succeed—Proverbs 16:3.

Do you know how wonderful it is to have time to have lunch with a friend or to spend an afternoon on the phone with a niece, nephew or daughter? To send a card to a lady of our church who recently lost a relative? This was my afternoon. I jumped out of the whirlwind that used to be my life filled with kindnesses that I was always going to do, words of encouragement that I was always going to share. I just went through a basket of cards. There were at least 30 that I bought with specific people in mind. I was going to send them, but got too busy to write the note inside. If good intentions pave the way to heaven, then I was on a superhighway! Do we recognize the trade off? Two TVs or time with a child or spouse… 2 cars or a quiet meal on the table with small talk and no one in a rush to leave… a new DVD or a calm bedtime hour to sit and tell stories to the children, creating memories that will last. Who would have ever thought a Type A personality could get so laid back? I am realizing true success in my life, a joy in living, loving and giving. We all have our jobs to do. I am not even hinting that we should not work.

But maybe it should only be a means. I could point out some major milestones in my career, in terms of both money and prestige. But why do I keep remembering a time when money was tight and we wanted a vacation? I stayed at home with our two teenagers and one preteen. Just the food on a vacation would have broken us. My husband came up with an idea of how to finance a vacation. If the kids could earn one-third of the money, then we would have a garage sale for one-third of the money, and then our savings would provide the final third. You never saw so much yard mowing, babysitting, and neighborhood odd jobs being done. We took off to the Wisconsin Dells. We even let our children manage the money. All I wanted was one healthy meal a day. I am chuckling now as I think of their making the decisions for each purchase and activity. On the final day of the vacation, they were deciding on whether to spend ten dollars each for an all-day water park pass (which meant we would have to drive home that night) or stay one more day and do less expensive things. We stayed one more day. Not once on that vacation did they ask us for anything. They were in charge. In fact, I don't remember any souvenir buying. You know, if I had been working, we would have had enough money to indulge their every wish. But would I have had this precious memory? Maybe schools should have lessons on the value of time spent together, that less *can* be more. We have shared this story many times with friends and relatives as the kids gathered around on the holidays.

Lord, thank you for the tears of joy that You are giving me now. Your blueprints for success are so much broader than what I had planned.

Thank You!

13

Questions? Questions? Questions?

Two gas company servicemen, a senior training supervisor and a young trainee, were out checking meters in a suburban neighborhood. They parked their truck at one end of the alley and worked their way to the other end. At the last house, an older woman was looking out her window watching the two men as they checked her gas meter. Finishing the meter check, the senior supervisor challenged his younger coworker to a foot race down the alley and back to the truck to prove that an older guy could outrun a younger one. As they came running up to the truck, they realized that the lady from that last house was huffing and puffing right behind them. They stopped and asked her what was wrong. Gasping for breath, she replied, "When I see two gas men running as hard as you two were, I figure I'd better run too.

I laugh when I hear a child laugh. I don't have to know what the laughing is about. I have seen two people hug with tears in their eyes, and I well up. Don't have to know why. And I definitely could have been that woman. This gives me cause to think about who is watching me and what their reactions might be. Do I reflect hope or despair? So many circumstances come to mind. Bobbie, my friend, and I were having a 2-hour breakfast… we have a lot to talk about. We had laughed so hard we were crying, (Bobbie, Beth and I are the only ones I know who can be laughing hysterically one moment and have it turn into convulsive crying immediately. I never said we were sane.) An older couple came over to us and told us that they had been watching us the whole time. They said we had made their day.

They were laughing right along with us and said they appreciated observing such a friendship.

I sometimes wonder what I would I have thought had I seen Jesus, in the flesh, walk by. How would I have reacted? Would I have followed? Did He heal everyone He passed by, or was it just the ones who asked? Was there anyone who asked that He continued to pass by? Did He have compassion for everyone? Who caused Him the most problems? Would I have been like a Pharisee? Would the traditions and legalism of my teachings blind me to the very source of my beliefs? I am sure you have many questions of your own. Would the questions now be any different from the questions they had then?

Lord, shine a flashlight on my heart and mind. Let me see the corners of doubt and disbelief. Help others to observe

You living in me. You are my strength and salvation. Let Your Holy Spirit fill every speck of my life. Amen.

14

1413 Euca.... Oak

When the elderly gentleman realized his wife was having a heart attack he quickly dialed 911. The operator asked him his street address. He stated 1413 S. Eucalyptuses. Then the operator asked him to spell the street name. There was a long pause… then the gentleman asked the operator, "Could you pick her up on Oak?" "O.A.K., it is one street over and I can drag her there."

Remember when you were young and naive? I became a Christian at the age of 14. I had heard theologies and "religious talk" my whole childhood. I knew exactly what "we" believed—scripture and verse. I also knew why I did not belong to other denominations—scripture and verse. Somewhere in this transition I had developed a sense of "*I was right so "they" must be wrong*" theology. I boldly shared this with my then best friend, Peggy. We would meet after school and on weekends to play games, share snacks and ideas. It was time for Peggy to enter Catechism at her church and after each class she would tell me all that she had learned. I was amazed at how many things we believed alike. On one such occasion, she asked me if I believed in the Triune Godhead. Now, understand, I was 14. Her beliefs had been discussed in our home and I knew her teachings were considered waaaay more liberal than our family's. So I asked her whether she did or not. She said "Yes." I figured if she believed it, then I must not! So I said "No." I had heard the term Trinity and Three-in-One but never Triune Godhead. I used to look back with embarrassment on that episode, but now it has become a reminder that there is more than one way to express a truth. God did not stamp us out all alike. Some worship with clapping hands. Some love the Doxology. Some listen for the "still small voice," while others are looking for signs. There are seminaries that propagate Calvinism, while other seminaries teach the thoughts of Wesley. Where is the seminary that says that both teachings can co-exist? Am I still naïve to think that God doesn't care so much how you dot the "I" as much as how we respect each other's differences and how we walk the path set before us? The devil has to smile every time he sees us swell with pride because "We know the truth." I have no fear in stating what I believe, but I walk with fear and trembling about the spirit in which my message is given.

Lord, I love to worship You! I love the music You have given that brings a tear to my eyes and comfort to my soul. I cherish the markers from the past where You have made Yourself known.

15

A Firm Foundation

It has been said that the Main Library at Indiana University sinks over an inch every year because when it was built, engineers failed to take into account the weight of all the books that would occupy the building.

I look at the building that God gave me, and for some reason, I can relate to that library. I must have been designed for a lot less food, and I definitely was not built to take on the weight of the world. But, for some reason, I keep on trying. Gil was in the choir. I was teaching a class on discipleship and our two teens were in the youth group. At least Steve, our preteen, was not yet involved. One typical Sunday evening, we were rushing to get each of us to our appropriate spots on time. It was wonderful to finally have two cars to split this responsibility. So off we went, each enjoying an evening at church. When we started to leave the church, no one could find Steve. We had everyone looking for him until his teacher told us he never came to class. It was then Gil and I turned to each other and realized neither of us had brought him. We had a neighbor whose son would come to our house and Steve would play at their house. Then I realized Steve had gone over that afternoon and we had not picked him up.

Do you know how embarrassing it is to tell your neighbor that you forgot your kid! Steve was having a great time but was a little concerned that he had missed church. He has become the most organized of all of us. I see him plan his finances and I am sure Old Abe Lincoln screams every time he comes out of Steve's pocket. Steve sets goals of where he wants to be in his life, and he is not easily swayed from those goals. I believe he knows that God is the foundation for all his decision-making, then any surprises will not cause him to sink inch by inch like the library. As for me, the times I feel like my feet are on quicksand and I am sinking fast, are the times I know I got in the way of God's plans. I try to make everything and everyone "all right," when all along maybe God just wants to keep piling on more books so he can develop a firmer foundation. Lord, I know that I am not the cure-all. I know I cannot make everyone OK. But then why do I try so hard? I can only lift each one in prayer. Today, my prayer is the prayer of Serenity.

Lord, help me to change the things I can, to accept the things I cannot change, and give me the wisdom to know the difference. Amen.

16

If the Shoe Fits!

From the Mayo Clinic Health Letter: Try this shoe test on shoes that you have at home. Stand barefoot on a piece of paper and have someone trace the outline of your shoe over that of your foot. If your foot outline is wider than your shoe width, your shoes are too small.

You don't have to look very far to find humor. I keep thinking of my granddaughters clanking around in high heels that are way too big. They pretend to be all grown up and they think they look beautiful. And my grandson has a fisherman's hat that keeps flopping over one eye, but he knows he is cool! Come to think of it, I even have some clothes that I keep trying to squeeze myself into. Maybe those instructions aren't that ridiculous. I sometimes imagine God sitting in a great big comfy chair looking down through white fluffy clouds and just observing His children. "Look at little Joe over there, he thinks all that money is his." "And look at Sally over there, she is trying so hard to be perfect." "Didn't Susie hear me tell her to go help John?" "Jim, you have prayed that same prayer every day this month, I heard you the first time." I know we have had a pattern of footprints made for each of us.

Psalms 119:105 comes to mind… Your word is a lamp unto my feet and a light for my path. Now this is a shoe that fits! We keep asking God for direction and help and maybe even new instructions, when all along the footsteps are there in His Word. All we have to do is find out what fits.

I love talking to you, God. Does it bother You that I ask so many questions that You have already answered? I look at my grandbabies and think of all the questions that they keep asking over and over. Is it the same with You? Are you enjoying my walk? Do I ever make You impatient? Do You wish I were a faster learner? Are my shoes too tight or too big? Illuminate Your light unto my path. Thank You for the shoes You have so magnificently made-to-order just for me. Help me to put them on with love.

17

Two Ears To Hear

It's said that there is an average of 178 sesame seeds on a McDonald's Big Mac bun.

Now I don't know who did all the counting, but whoever it was has way too much time on their hands. Unless you are allergic to or have a fetish for sesame seeds, then who really cares? Someone out there thinks we should know all this useless information. I am amazed at how many of my own friends sent this to me. It even seemed interesting to me when I read it. I am grateful for my friends and all the information they share that adds nothing to my life. I know when every friend's grandchild pooped like a grownup for the first time. I know how hard it is for some to grow fingernails. I even know who looks better in purple, and those that glow when they wear red. Why do we do this to each other? I am still giving a play by play of when my rash breaks out, the severity of it, and my theories of its origin. My goodness, I guess I never realized how patient my friends really are. What is it that binds us together? Why would so many want me to know about Big Mac buns? Maybe it is in part the listening and being heard. Strangest of all is that I really do care. If it makes them happy, it makes me happy.

If something causes them sadness, then I want to help them. I wonder why God thought it was important for us to know that He has counted every hair on our heads? Or that He cares for the lilies of the fields? They don't have a soul, do they? They are mainly there to be enjoyed. Does He enjoy his own handiwork? I am glad He cares and listens. All of a sudden, I feel a sense of being cared for and appreciated. I just saw a man named "Bone" who changed his life around because the Nightline host, Ted Koppel, listened to him when he was a gang member in the L.A. gangs. He was expressing that when Ted interviewed him, it was the first time he felt heard about the things that were important to him. Ted helped him reflect on what he was doing with his life. That was when he realized how destructive his life had become and he needed to make changes. How many other "Bones" are out there that just need an ear and a little direction?

Lord, you gave me two ears. Help me to put them to service. Help me to hear past the words and into the hearts of those You love. There is no one who does not have value. Help me to affirm those around me. Use me to show them that You care.

18

"Pig!"

A man was driving on a narrow, winding mountain road when he almost collided with a car wildly careening around a blind curve. "You stupid fool!" he shouted at the other driver. The other car came to a dead stop. A woman rolled down the window, looked at the man and yelled, "Pig!" and then quickly drove off. Furious at the insult, the man slammed his car into gear, roared around the mountain curve and slammed head on into a giant hog standing in the road.

There must be an art to listening or being heard. Screaming wasn't the answer. Urgency wasn't the answer. She told him the truth and that wasn't enough. Why did he not see that she was not a fool but a desperate person? Why did she not give a full explanation, "There is a pig in the road ahead"? It is all semantics! I have faced lions and tigers and bears. I have turned on sirens of impending tornadoes, hurricanes and floods, sometimes to no avail. On our family website, we have been debating the issue of submission and the dynamics it creates in both our culture and the Asian cultures. You can't begin to imagine the times we have had to take the words and break them down just to be understood. No, aggressive and vocal are not the same, nor are meek and passive. Yes, a vocal person can be meek and submissive. From now on I am just going to yell, "Pig in the road!" when I don't understand or if I feel misunderstood. Of course, that could be taken wrong too, couldn't it? It seems that assumptions and expectations cause us the biggest problems in life. Since we started the website, one brother in his 60s stated that his perception of each of us had changed. He had this notion of who we were and what we were about. Throughout the family interaction, the depth of what we were and what we wanted were not expressed to its fullest. I would challenge you to keep a journal (I am sure that was a new thought) of who you are and what you are about. You see, I think we all want to be known for who we are. I think there are situations in every family that have caused hurts and seem beyond repair. If only we would just take the time to listen from "their" viewpoint and try to understand "their" expectations. Moms and dads don't want to be "dictators"! Children don't want to be perceived as "rebellious"! Siblings don't like the word "rivalry"! Who likes the word "gossip"? What is it really about?

Lord, You never have to say "Pig in the road." You understand.

I want to be more like You. You challenge us in Your Word to seek wisdom and understanding. But, I also know that with each gift comes responsibility. Help me to be wise with each relationship. Help me to see past the obvious and get to what is real.

19

Warnings

It may be that your sole purpose in life is simply to serve as a warning to others—Monday morning chuckle.

What a thought provoker! All of a sudden, I am envisioning clanging bells and red flashing lights at a railroad crossing. I know God has given each of us purpose, and I have been in many a seminar looking for mine, but to end up being just a warning would really be depressing. I just saw a movie called "28 Days" with Sandra Bullock. She was in rehab to overcome alcohol and drug abuse. Now, she definitely could have been labeled "WARNING." I know of a pastor who left his church when his congregation continually confronted him about the slipshod way they thought he ran the church's business. He could have listened and changed, or they could have helped take up the slack—WARNING. I know a young mother with three children under five who had an exceptionally frazzled day. She had planned a special day with her children but instead she was waylaid by an emergency with a business partner and spent the whole morning getting him medical help. When things calmed down, she stopped at a Target store to get a diaper for her one-year-old. Anyone downwind knew he had a definite problem. The two other children were hanging from the shopping cart, and she knew they needed to get home for a nap.

When lo and behold, within five minutes through the store and to the checkout, she had three separate people chastise her about the children. On the verge of tears, and with three children hanging from her body, she finally reached her car. One of the women who had approached her inside, followed her to the car and handed her a Gospel tract. Did she really think that is what she needed at that moment? —WARNING. We can look at many situations in our lives and the lives of others and see warning signals going nonstop!

WARNING—Go Help! WARNING—Give! WARNING—Don't! WARNING—I need to talk to you! WARNING—Doesn't that hurt?!

It is so much easier to look at others and wonder how they ever missed the warnings and wonder what could they possibly have been thinking. Personally, I would rather learn a lesson by observation versus experience.

So Lord, I am watching and listening. You have given my life purpose. Use me to be an expression of Your love. Use me to help others. And if You must, then use me as a warning. Wait…. is that a red light flashing?

20

A Sheep in Cat's Clothing

Tennis rackets are strung with steel or nylon, but some are still made out of sheep guts. Many string instruments use sheep guts as their mainstay. You could even see sheep guts used in surgical sutures and, gulp, sausage casings.

Am I the only one who had heard it called "Cat Guts"? Where do all those old tales originate? I am beginning to question my own reality. There is an old story that has been passed around about a mother who, every time she would bake a ham, would slice approximately an inch off each end before putting it in a roaster. When this practice was questioned by her newly married daughter, the mother explained that she had always done that because that is how her mother had taught her. So, mother and daughter went off to see grandma and asked her why she always cut the ends of the ham by 1 inch. To the grandmother's amusement, she explained that was the only way it would fit in her small roaster all those years. What an awesome responsibility we have as parents! I could talk until I am blue in the face about principles of life that I want to teach my children. But it seems that my actions just keep getting in the way. Have your kids ever told you that you think you are perfect? Have they ever confronted you and said that you act like you never make mistakes? Were they not listening? I know I have owned up to a couple of mistakes! How about that "LAST WORD?" Is there anyone in the house who seems to own it? Isn't it ridiculous some of the patterns we have established as a family? If it weren't for the occasional tears in my eyes, I would tell you how funny it is to observe some of the interactions of my family and how, as adults, each has come to the interesting conclusion about what they believe to be true. You could give me any topic and I could ramble on about it for hours. I know that is why my daughter won so many speech contests—she got that from me. Now, her tendency for arguing, I am sure is from her father. I love physical activity, and both of the boys love sports—they got that from me. Now that compelling desire to win must have been from their father. They each have a great appreciation for humor. I love a good laugh. They must have gotten that from me also, but the constant teasing—that's from their father. Yes, I am jesting, but why am I so proud when I see them full of compassion, love, laughter and all the great qualities, but cringe when I see in them self-centeredness and stubbornness, and all those negative traits that keep raising their ugly heads? Does it hit home too much? Do I see the worst of me before my eyes?

Here we go again, Lord. Maybe if they see me praying it will outweigh all those times I was seeking my own way. Forgive me if I appear to have all the answers. When I am trying to do things right, am I just trying to make things go the way I want them to? Introspection hurts sometimes. Here I am in my fifties. You would think I would be doing more teaching than learning. Lord, You can be so funny. It seems that now I am learning from my children. Their actions speak volumes. Help me to be a quick and humble student.

21

Christian Incognito

Common oxymorons: small crowd, peace force, plastic glasses, act naturally, good grief, pretty ugly, working vacation, exact estimate, same difference, jumbo shrimp, alone together, genuine imitation and airline food!

How about lazy Christian, prejudiced Christian, foul-mouthed Christian, Christian incognito. There are just some words that don't make sense when they are put together. When I became a child of God, I added the name of Christian to my repertoire of identities. This gives me concern about how many times I have become a living oxymoron. I can't seem to get Philippians 4:6-8 out of my mind. (Why does God do this to me so much?) Let's see, whatever is true, noble, right, pure, lovely, admirable, excellent or praiseworthy—think about such things. Now I wonder which category I would fit in while I was at the Mayo Clinic. Wait a minute! Now all I can think of is 1 Cor. 13:4-7: Love is patient, kind, does not envy, does not boast, is not proud or rude or self-seeking. It is not easily angered, keeps no record of wrongs nor delights in evil but rejoices with truth. It always protects, always trusts, always hopes and always perseveres.

As a Christian, am I as patient as Job? Don't want to find out! I guess you could ask my husband if I keep records of wrong. I don't believe I do until he does the same stupid thing over and over, and then I can't help but remember. He keeps reminding me. Now, I don't believe I delight in evil, but when I watch TV, I sure am glad when the bad guys get their due. And I will guarantee you that there isn't a situation that I have been in where I have not tried to get to the truth of the matter. What about always trusts? Who is it we are to trust? Is everyone trustworthy? Am I accountable for my trust or their trustworthiness? Now, this is getting a little hard. I love the word "easily" in front of angered. It does make a difference, you know. It gives me a little out. I can allow for a few cars in front of me on the highway, but if I am in traffic longer than an hour, maybe I have a right to a little indignation. Look how many times "always" is used. Not sometimes or now and then but ALWAYS protect, trust, hope and persevere. Protect what? Lives? Good names and reputations? Innocence?

Lord, this walk You have given me sure does take a lot of thought. I keep feeling the need to justify so many of my actions. I want to bear Your name and yet I know I have not ALWAYS lived up to Your ideals.

I know You alone are my hope and only You can help me to persevere, but some of the rest of those traits I will have to work on a little harder. My desire is to be like You!

22

The Phone Call

An office reports that they have an answering machine that instructs callers to leave their name and address and to spell any difficult words. Early one Monday, while the secretary was reviewing the weekend messages, she heard an enthusiastic young woman recite her name and address and then confidently offer, "My difficult word is reconciliation. R-E-C-O-N-C-I-L-I-A-T-I-O-N."

You know, it is not only a hard word to spell, it is also difficult to achieve. I watched "Survivors" last night on TV. They required a man to eat three fat live worms that had really ugly head. If he did so, he would be eligible for one million dollars. I could not, would not, should not do such a thing. But sometimes it is as difficult to mend wounded spirits. Have you ever had the responsibility of organizing a church-sponsored event? You had better have a steel breastplate and the Lord with you or you shouldn't do it! If your events have always run smoothly, then please write me. I want to meet you. I have yet to meet an angel in person. We loved challenging the teenagers in our youth group by having parties that required a lot of interaction. One favorite was dressing up in costumes that represented their favorite missionary country, and then bringing a food native to that country. I am still not sure what kind of meat the guy with the bone in his hair brought. Every time we stuck it with a fork, it would bleed green. Could not, would not, should not! There were times it took two hours of clues just to find where the party was being held. What has this to do with broken spirits? We had a couple of people who would love to help… sometimes. Every time an event was being planned, we would receive "the phone call". There always seemed to be a concern. Was there going to be a spiritual aspect to the party? How were the teens going to dress? Was it appropriate? Who were the chaperones? Were they spiritual? Would the older people in the church think it was OK? The discussion could go on for hours. I can look back and see the impatience that I showed. If there are two people making a decision, then of course, there are going to be two ideas. Invariably, weeks following each function, we had a worship service that would bring conviction and the lady who made "the phone call" would come and ask my forgiveness. The first couple of times I didn't know what she was asking forgiveness for. She would then let me know that before each party she called around and talked about what we were planning to make sure everyone was OK with it.

She worried that she had been a little gossipy. I must tell you she is a beautiful woman and I love her dearly. But we both had some lessons to learn. I believe that her main desire in life was to please the Lord. But she had a hard time with us. She lived a very conservative life and she was always afraid that someone would sit in judgment of each activity, and that they might get upset with her. After an hour of each conversation, I was always thoroughly exasperated. It took me days to wind down, and I may not have fit in the category of "to be angry and sin not." Nor can I say I always forgave her with a pure heart. That was 25 years ago and we are still friends today. We see each other a couple of times a year. She now has freedom in her service to the Lord. I believe we have mutual respect for each other because of our willingness to mend the words and hurts that we had caused each other. I admire the tenderness she has in her love for the Lord and her willingness to humble herself to make amends. Hopefully, I have become a gentler spirit also.

I am grateful for the people You have put in my life, Lord. So many of them are so easy to love. Help me to be aware that when people seem to be irritating, they could be used by You as a sharpening stone. I have not always loved them in the way that You do. Forgive me. Help me to always have the spirit of R-E-C-O-N-C-I-L-I-A-T-I-O-N!

23

God Made Me Woman

If He can talk through an ass, then let God talk through me!

Church, you won't let me be a pastor. You discourage me from being a preacher. You even plant doubts of my capability of teaching a grown man any of God's ways. So, why this gift that God has given me? When *do* I use it? I write those thoughts and ideas that I believe God has poured out to me. You see, I love God with all that is within me and I believe that He has given me some insights that need to be shared. May I only share them with women? Is there wisdom that I may share with everyone? Share with men, women, children, anyone who would seek out thoughts and ideas that will assist them in their spiritual growth. I thank God for a forum where you can get past what I look like or who I am, and realize that I am no more or no less than one more voice crying in the wilderness. I have such a love for you that I ache with a desire to share with you a part of my walk in God's classroom. I do not yet have my crown, but I have received some stars that might make my crown a bit prettier when I reach home. Is there a woman in your family whom you regard as assertive, aggressive or rebellious? Or one who seems to have no desire to be under "anyone's" authority?

Take a moment and visualize the actions of those women. Why? Why would they set themselves up to be perceived as angry or frustrated? I suggest that we take a closer look and not just attribute these actions to a worldly motivation. Scripture tells us that we all have gifts of the Spirit. Are they all for men and women? It would be so much easier if all the women had the gifts of service, hospitality and mercy and all the men had the teaching, preaching and exhorting gifts. But that isn't the way God planned it. I don't know which would be more challenging in the church, a man with the gift of mercy or a woman with the gift of prophecy. Was I behind the door when You passed out that meek and quiet spirit to all the women, Lord?

I know that everyone would be more loving and accepting of me if I were doing more physical serving and a lot less talking. So many years I have tried to fit in that box that others have made for me. Forgive me. It is not the acceptance of others that I desire. You have plenty of voices here on Earth, but if You need one more, then here I am. Do not let Your messenger get in the way of anyone hearing Your voice. Lord, I pray for wisdom.

24

Pressure Escapes

Women invented bulletproof vests, fire escapes, windshield wipers and laser printers. You go girls! If necessity is the mother of invention, then I wonder what was going on in the lives of those women who invented bulletproof vests and fire escapes. Who sits around thinking, "How could I protect myself from a bullet"? I must admit the thought has never crossed my mind! Now the fire escape is another matter. Can't you picture all the uses for a fire escape? Of course, fire is my first thought. Haven't had an illicit affair, and if I sang the songs from West Side Story, the gang itself would kill me. (Wait, where is that vest?) Come to think of it, I have never even been on a fire escape. Now, I don't know whether to be grateful or whether I should go looking for one. I guess I could sit here and think of all the other things from which we would like to escape. Pressure would be one. We already have medicines and placebos to help alleviate some of the pressures of life. How about giving a pressure course in school? Every community could have a specific walk, only to be used when you need to release pressure. If you want to throw a tantrum, there would be pots to throw and (make-believe) cats to kick. We would hire a counselor to be there 24 hours a day, if you need to talk. Kleenex would be strewn along the path. We would even build a wailing wall. Maybe there would be a bullhorn or two for those who just have to shout. And at the end, we will have a cage for those of us who get completely out of control and could use some restraint. I guess I am too late though. Don't we already have a pressure escape? Why do we need to invent more when we don't always use the resources we already have? Have you ever just listed the names of God? Counselor, Prince of Peace, Almighty God! By the time you ponder each name that He is called and have faith in the very meaning of His names, surely some of the pressure will be gone. Why did I learn so quickly how to escape a fire, but keep forgetting where to go for other emergencies? Is it easier to take a pill or let our bodies just fall apart than to release our pressures to God? Do we look more for an escape versus prevention so we don't have to change the way we live? When was the very first breakdown recorded in history? Or, is all this pressure just a 20th-century phenomenon? Adam and Eve knew where to go! So did Noah and Abraham! Look up David.... now he deserved a breakdown!

Lord, why do some of us have to be broken before You get our attention? All we have to do is come to You and You will give us rest. We look for antidotes and cures and do what the doctors and teachers instruct us to do. Instead, maybe we should just be looking for the root of our pressures. I know only You can truly restore the damage that stress has created. Forgive me for trying to pick up the load by myself. I know You are there waiting to carry it with me. Here, please take this load and prod me when I start to take it back again. Amen.

25

Soul Weary

Psalm 119:28 My soul is weary with sorrow; strengthen me according to Your word.

This is God's answer to my call today. How did He know? I can't think of a more appropriate word than weary. Could a child of 10 or 16 or even 20 experience weary? I see the word wear inside of the word weary and realize that I am worn out. Have you ever had someone express a hurt to you that was caused by a third party? And we love both parties. What is one to do? Scripture tells us not to take up another's offense. Honestly, I don't want to. I can suggest that both parties talk it over and come to a conclusion. That would work fine if they would both be willing. But, what if one is and one is not? What if that third party just plain does not like the first? Scripture tells us to love each other, but what about liking each other? You know, there are some people who make it very difficult to like them. Does that create "an offense" by not liking someone? When you are around them they cause chaos. I understand trying to eliminate stress and chaos in our lives, but we are back to those hard-to-love people again. God tells us not to "weary" in doing what is good. You would think that doing what is good would only uplift you. But that is not always the case.

Not everyone receives your good with a pure heart. That brings me to the sorrow. On one side, I see someone who is their own worst enemy and so out of control because of such a strong need for acceptance and unconditional love, that the very thing that they need the most is being destroyed. On the other side, I see a "stiffness of neck," a person who is so protective and controlling of her own life that the flaws in others are only one more reason not to be involved. And here I sit, trying to make peace that only God can give. What message have I sent? One person believes that I can help solve a dilemma and another one wonders why I don't understand the shun. I read an article the other day stating that if you are asked for advice, do not give it unless you can keep the person from dying, but even then, think twice. Of course, that was not from scripture. All I know how to do is to help each person to look within himself and find his own peace with God without trying to change anyone else. Lord, what about the shun? I have read that even the Amish shun those who don't conform to their teachings. But then, how would we reach the lost? Did Jesus shun anyone? I know my love for others comes from You, but I can think of those I may tend to avoid because they make life more stressful for me.

We already live in too stressful a society with way too many diseases that are a consequence of stress.

Lord, convict my heart. Show me when to walk away from turmoil and guide me when I can be of help to others. I know it is not as difficult as I seem to make it.

26

The Enabler

But God was with him and rescued him from all his troubles. He gave Joseph wisdom and enabled him… Acts 7:9b, 10a

If I were a preacher, I would illustrate so many points from this verse in my sermon that I could put Rip Van Winkle back to sleep. Have you ever enjoyed a quiet time with the Lord, reading His word, and a verse just won't go away? You try to go on. You really want to finish the chapter, but you keep going back to one particular verse. Well, I can't get away from this verse today. I kept trying to pick it apart to see what God wanted to show me. Of course, I started by acknowledging that God was with me also. Isn't that thought awesome? How could I be lonely? How could I sin? How could I not love? How could I pass up a need? You see, God is with me! I believe I could have dwelt on those thoughts for hours and gained all kinds of insights, but that wasn't what God was showing me. So I went on. God rescued him from all his troubles. I really wanted this to be the message for me today. Just think of it. God was doing it all! Can you imagine? Poof! I have no more troubles or enemies. None! Let's see if I can make a list. What gives me the most trouble? 1. Discipline. I fight with Him all the time.

2. Time. I try my best to enjoy and make the best use of my time, but the saying is truer than ever, *"time is fleeting."* Wait, this isn't where God was leading me either. Now here is the good stuff. God gave Joseph wisdom and enabled him. Do the two go hand in hand? James tells us that if we ask, God will give generously of His wisdom. Since the first time I read this in James, I have included it as part of my prayer life. But so is "Thank You for this food. Amen." I believe that God was showing me it was not a mere add on. He told me to bless my food, so I bless my food. He told me to ask for wisdom, so I ask for wisdom. How do I keep turning into a Pharisee? I start out with a new truth and a deep desire to do God's will, and the next thing you know it all turns into rituals. The true meaning or an expectancy of certain results get lost in the very redundancy of the request. I want wisdom that enables me. God enables me. That is what He showed me today. He gives me His power. He gives me His ability. God is my enabler!

Right now, Father, I feel as if I can do anything while You are teaching me. Wait, I take that back. I know I can do anything with You as You give me wisdom and enable me. I ask to grow in wisdom and stature.

I have heard the word "enabler" used in such a negative context with so much psychobabble recently that it has lost its powerful, positive meaning. Thank You, thank You, again, I say thank You, Father.

27

Selective Weakness

The weaker sex is the stronger sex because of the weakness of the stronger sex for the weaker sex.

I love the person who said this! It is exactly how I talk. What is this weak and strong stuff? When Gil and I go shopping, he always carries all the bags. I have always appreciated this gesture, and it sure makes shopping more fun. Go ahead and call me weaker. I have a terrible time opening jars. I just can't grip them like Gil can. Yep, I am weaker. But if I need the furniture moved, I will wait until he leaves for work. I have actually moved an entertainment center and bunk beds from one room to another. You see, he grumbles. If I were to ask him to move the couch to the other side of the room, the first comment would be, why? Then, after moving it and I see I don't like it there and really want it somewhere else, you would think the Bears had lost a Super Bowl of some kind. Aaghhhh! And that would stop me from having a thought of a third placement for that couch. Come to think of it, that just shows how smart Gil really is. I remember one night when we had put the kids to bed and had just settled down, and there was a loud noise outside our bedroom window. We both lay there and listened intently to try and figure out what it was.

But it got louder and louder. We never had weapons in our home when the children were little, but Gil always kept a baseball bat by the bed. (He believes in being prepared and you never know when someone might want to play. Just joking!) He told me to stay put as he took the bat with him to the front door. In the meantime, I hurried to the kitchen and got my trusty butcher knife in case someone tried to attack him. As he went out the door, he heard a noise behind him, and not knowing it was me, he started to swing his bat. At the same time I was raising my knife. We saw how ridiculous we both looked and broke out with hysteria. If there had been a burglar, he must have realized right then and there that those idiots don't have anything I want. In fact, we might have even looked dangerous. So it isn't just the need to protect that makes one stronger, because I am just as protective of him as he is of me. Maybe vulnerable would fit here. Am I more vulnerable to harm? The verse from Peter that this weak and strong thing was based on continues to admonish us women not to give in to fear. I do believe that we sometimes fret over the everyday things more than men do. Gil has never worried if we had at least eight plates or a set of silverware with the same pattern. I catch him all the time putting on black shoes with brown pants. And he honestly did not care who we invited to our children's weddings—just as long as he was told what time to show up and that there would be enough food for him. Maybe that is why the Lord told men to be considerate of their wives and to treat them with respect and love them so that nothing would hinder their prayers. Sometimes they just don't understand the inner workings of the home for a woman and how so many of the little things are important to her. Lord, I know Gil doesn't care if he crawls into pink or blue sheets at night, and he doesn't have a clue what makes them so soft and smell so good. I sometimes even wonder how often they would get changed if I weren't around. He isn't even sure what it is I do that has turned our house into a home, but I know he definitely feels the love that is lavished on each endeavor.

Lord, help me follow Peter's counsel, to do what is right and not give way to fear. And Lord, I lift Gil up to You. I want You to hear his prayers also. He doesn't have to understand me. Just help him to respect my need to fuss and fret.

28

Disabling Expectations

Adversity introduces a man to himself. —Practical Proverbs & Wacky Wit

Tell me about Helen Keller's mother. I hope someone was holding Helen's mother when she cried. I have seen the shows and books on the life of Helen Keller and heard many admirable things about her life, but I want to know about her mother. How did she deal with the hurts and disappointments? Did she ever love Helen completely and unconditionally? How did she cope with giving up control to another woman, Anne Sullivan, her teacher? I can't imagine being in her shoes. How long would it have taken before I realized the miracle that Helen had become? If it's God's will that is leading us, then how can we label anything a disability or hardship? Some challenges may be easier to bear and accept than others, but are our lives still in the hands of God even when things appear disastrous? Could it possibly be that those who appear to be whole are really the ones who are made to have a harder and longer time to overcome their own "disability"? There are words that can only be completely understood through experience such as: pain and sorrow, embarrassment, compassion, humility, pride and victory.

Would not each of us have to go through the process of being different to make these words come alive? My husband, Gil, was born with just two fingers and a thumb on his left hand. Did his mom cry? If she did, it would not have been for herself. He would quickly tell you that he is the only one who is "normal" and all the rest of us are different. He would even challenge anyone to clean out the bottom of a jar or glass as quickly or as well as he can. He can use a computer, play ball and even hold my hand with the best of them! If you were to ask me, I would tell you that his "handicap" played a large role in giving him a heart as big as Wyoming. We all seem to have a record of expectations that keeps playing in our heads, and when those expectations are not met, we become disappointed, sometimes even to the point of depression. From where do these expectations stem? Not God! What is His idea of a perfect child? A perfect spouse? A perfect lifestyle? Abraham, Isaac and Jacob didn't even have a car! Moses worked all his life with the expectation of seeing the Promised Land. Did it happen? And that thorn in Paul's side? Some say it was a speech impediment. Others say he had trouble with his eyes and then of course, there is the one about it being his wife. Whatever, was it God's idea of perfection?

Father, I need to see that in Your eyes, there are no disabilities. When I see someone who is different, help me not only to be understanding, but also to surround this person's whole family with hugs and prayers. I am grateful for the many blessings You have given me, and I will do my best to live a life of contentment. Love Ya!

29

Black, White and Gray

The truth will set you free—but first it will make you mad.
—Practical Proverbs.

Have I told you how much I enjoy being with our grandchildren? I seem to understand children so much more than I did when mine were little. The other night, our oldest granddaughter, Andie, and Papaw were having a great time with the paints. They had suns and moons and trees and some indistinguishable animals all over the construction paper. Then it turned into a face painting party. The giggling became contagious, and I had to go and join them. When they finished, Papaw proudly told Andie to sign her masterpieces like all creative artists do, and we would put them on the fridge. Then my lesson began. As Papaw started helping her to sign her name on all her artwork, Andie began crying. You knew she was frustrated. She kept telling us that was not her name. She shook her head, telling us to make it right. Papaw kept asking her what was wrong because we all knew her name was Andie, but that wasn't working. Then it dawned on me that he was using all capitals. Had she never seen her name as ANDIE? She is only four. Maybe she had only seen it as Andie. Sure enough, she calmed down when we wrote it "right." It had not only frustrated her, it had hurt her feelings that we did not know how to write her name. I am going to go out and buy myself a pin that is a replica of a gray crayon for my suits, because I need something to be a reminder to me when I respond as Andie did. I, too, see most of my world from the point of reference of what I have been taught or experienced. I make so many judgments on the basis of being right or wrong and black or white. I admire, and am envious of, those who see things as being different or creative without any judgment whatsoever.

I do not want to be a stumbling block, but let me share an example. All our daughter's school friends were getting their ears pierced in their early teens. We had informed Beth that she would have to wait until she was 18. I had attended a church where we were taught that wearing jewelry was sinful, and my mother and many of my friends still held that belief as a truth. Even though the church we then attended did not hold to the same teaching, and I had my own thoughts on the subject, I respected their belief system and did not want to be a stumbling block. Plus, I did not want to approve of something with which later on Beth might have a problem. Beth did get her ears pierced at 18. I waited until I was 50. You can't believe how cute Andie is with her little earring collection, at age 4. My mother has not changed from her teaching, and that is OK. This is where I get to take out my gray crayon. I don't need to change her. Now I may need to get her a gray crayon also. She doesn't need to change me. Believe me, I love the Lord! And so does Mom!

Lord, you tell us to work out our salvation with fear and trembling. Now I know salvation is by faith, so what am I to believe? Could it be that my walk is for me and me alone? That You will give us Your Holy Spirit to lead and to guide? Help me to not make judgments for anyone else. You have given me enough of my own truth to work through. Help me to be receptive as You broaden and complete Your truth in me. Amen

30

A Name Above All Names

Matthew 1:23b—and they will call Him Immanuel—which means, "God be with us."

Sometimes I am in such turmoil trying to be respectful and at the same time express what is real to me. Do you ever wonder how to address God when you are talking to Him? I have notice that when I write a prayer, I will use His title of Lord, but I usually don't talk that way. We call the example He gave to us the "Lord's Prayer," and yet it starts out with "Our Father… hallowed be Thy name." In English today, "hallowed" would mean "consecrate" or "revere." The dictionary defines God's name as to show honor and devotion and to worship and adore. I have always gone by my middle name of Diane, but my first name is Garnet. I used to wonder how my parents could have been so cruel. It was the name of one of my aunts who had a real struggle in life. There was some kind of weird message being sent to her that, even though you have made a mess of your life, there might still be hope. Now that is a heavy one to lay on someone. At some point, my family decided that they would call me by Diane. Anyone who goes by his or her middle name understands the constant confusion.

Every year in school there is the roll call. Again and again you have to explain, "No, I don't use the name Garnet, I use Diane." You have all the explaining to do to each kid in your class. Then there are the legal forms, first name, middle initial, last name. It is exhausting to forget my bank account number. Is it under G. Diane, Garnet D. or Garnet Diane? (You can see how severe my struggles are, can't you?) I think that if my Aunt Garnet were alive, she would be pleased with the meaning that has been placed on our name today. I remember when I was first called Garnet for real. Ronnie was our first daughter-in-law. Someday I am going to write about being the first of everything. It can be very difficult to break new ground, but it can also make you very special. Ronnie entered the terrain that every new family member seems to struggle over. What do we call our mother-in-law? One day, right out of the blue, Ronnie called me Garnet. Not just the name, but with a meaning that I cannot explain. It generated humor, and at the same time, tenderness and kindness. I don't know if she has ever realized how special she has made the name for me. I could never call my mother-in-law Mom. It seemed disrespectful to my own mother, but using her given name was disrespectful to her. My mother-in-law died young, and I never really did come to terms with an endearing name for her. I have two daughters-in-law now and when there is sharing of the closest kind, it seems they both get in the "Garnet" mood. It just doesn't take much to show a person that you love them. That is why I want a special name for God that the very sound of will give Him joy. Maybe that is why He has so many. The very pouring out of our soul can give Him His title.

Today I will call You Immanuel because You are with me. I know You are there each day, but today You seem even more special. I can't just say Immanuel, but I keep humming Your name. All of a sudden this has become a very special name for me to call You. Immanuel… hmmm… Immanuel. They call His name… hmmm… Immanuel…

31

That One Black Spot

Pleasant sights and good reports give happiness and health. Proverbs 15:30

Why is it so hard for some people to encourage others? How tiring these people can be. Just one small word can change a person's day for either good or bad. I remember a lesson I had shared years ago in a children's sermon. I took a large white poster board and with a black marker drew a small dot in the center. I then asked the kids what they saw. Most of the responses were that they saw a black dot. No one mentioned the obvious; the all white surface of the poster board. Do you see life that way? One small mistake or scar on one's life can get in the way of seeing what a precious and unique person God made each of us. The other day I stood in line for breakfast at McDonald's. Right beside me stood an 8- or 9-year-old girl, and she kept looking at me. I smiled, and then she told me that she thought I was beautiful and loved my purple outfit. I thanked her and let her know how kind she had been in telling me this. A small gesture from a child so warmed my heart and made my whole day enjoyable. I honestly looked around me all day to see if I too could find things about others to compliment and make the day better for them.

I envision my grandchildren running through my front door. Their eyes become as wide as their smiles. I immediately feel so much love for them that I am afraid my hugs will actually hurt them. Can you imagine feeling like that for everyone you see? I wonder if God ever wishes that he had physical arms to pull us to Him and just squeeze us until we could feel so much love that tears would come to our eyes. I wish He did. Can you even comprehend that kind of a hug? Maybe He gets just as much joy when He sees us loving each other. That smile on my face, the gleam in my eye, the extra bounce in my step. Can I take it with me wherever I go? How many times have I let that one little black dot of doubt or hurt squelch an opportunity to hug or be hugged?

Lord, I do feel Your presence. I am aware of Your handiwork everywhere I go. Forgive me for not living a life full of gratitude. Help me to embrace others full of Your love as I would my grandchildren.

32

The Unwrapped Gift

We have different gifts, according to the grace given us.
Romans 12:6

We all have it. That part of our lives that we kind of put on the back burner. We know it is there, but some form of apprehension prevents us from investigating every aspect of it. For some it is music. They just can't quit humming, or there is a tune that is always in the back of their minds. Maybe you are drawn to photography. You see this perfect picture that expresses so much, if only you had a camera. One day you will learn more about picture taking. You know it would be so pleasurable. So much emphasis seems to be put on learning basics of education and preparing for tests, without placing emphasis on the personal development of the creative gifts that are given to us. Why would we be so eager to put a child who is full of vinegar on some quiet pill rather than taking time with that child to see where all that energy could be directed in a more positive way? I have actually heard children being told that because they were so quiet, they were good children. I remember when I was growing up, we were often told "Children should be seen and not heard." Do we really want all children to be quiet?

It would make it easier to teach, but would it be better for each child? I remember a fifth-grade teacher telling me how much he loved my imagination and the stories I would write. I was in band all through high school. I sang in the choir. I loved art. I could hardly wait for each new craft that came out. Would all of this not have rung bells to the adults in my life that maybe I should work in the creative fields? Then, why was I encouraged to fit into the business world? Was it because that is where I could better support myself, and that was the field that was acceptable to everyone else around me? Was the business world supposed to define success for me? I think we pay a high price if we live a life defined by someone besides ourselves. If you are a teacher, parent, or any adult of influence, then you have a great responsibility to help children find the path that best suits them. I am going to do my best to affirm everyone I see. If I can help just one person unwrap the layers of false information and assumptions and get to the very core of who and what they are about, then I will have found success.

Lord, You talk about us being responsible for every idle word. I guess I had always assumed You were talking about gossip. But I realize that even putting negativity in another's life, or holding back from giving encouragement, can be displeasing to You. Help me to reach out and help those around me to unwrap the gifts You have given them.

33

Good Grief

To everything there is a season, a time to be born and a time to die. Ecc. 3:1.

Every book has a final chapter with a great and glorious conclusion. Mine, hopefully, is no exception. I didn't know why I left my writings lying around and untouched for six years until this summer. June 26, 2006, wasn't going to be anything special. We were going to enjoy a relaxing dinner and an otherwise uneventful evening. Just another day that would have soon been forgotten. You see, I don't remember what happened on April 26 or May 26, but I will always know, feel and ache for June 26. That is the day that Gil's spirit went to be with the Lord who he loved and adored throughout his life. There was not a warning, no good-bye, just one second he was here, and the next he had entered heaven. Through our 38 years together, we had many talks about "what if." We would laugh and tease about how the other would begin looking for a new mate, even at the funeral. I guarantee you, that was the last thing on my mind. But I want you to know about his funeral. We made it a celebration. Sharing the joy of knowing that Gil was experiencing more peace, rest, joy and love than he could ever have known here on Earth. One song that we sang was

"I bowed on my knees and cried Holy." Some of the words included "When I entered those gates of heaven, I saw Abraham, Isaac and Jacob and Paul and Timothy." Can you even imagine the depth of the thrill of experiencing that! I even envision him hugging his mom and dad and all the friends who have gone before. Hopefully he is even sitting with Roy Rogers, his very favorite cowboy. The song continues with "But I just want to see Jesus, the One who died for me. Then I bowed on my knees and cried, Holy, Holy, Holy…." How awesome! When I get to my lowest moments of missing him, I start singing this song, and I try to imagine the scope of the love that surrounds him. I realize that as much as I would love and cherish spending one more moment with him, it would be the last thing I would want for him now. It has been two months now and I realize how important the process of grieving has become. I have become more thankful for how I have been blessed. I am grateful for the friends who encourage and uplift me, and it makes me want to do even more for others who are hurting. I see the faces of widows and widowers, and I understand. Words that have been spoken throughout my life immediately become real. "Time is fleeting." "It is the little things that count." "Enjoy the moment." God, thank you for the life I shared with Gil and for the love that still remains with me, our children and all who knew Gil.

Thank you for the extra measure of grace that You have provided during this time of grieving. I feel Your presence so close now. I pray that this book, Gil's life, and my search for understanding may also inspire others to seek You and Your abundant love and everlasting presence. Lord, thank you. Amen.

Until we meet again. All my love, Diane

www.ingramcontent.com/pod-product-compliance
Lightning Source LLC
LaVergne TN
LVHW052048070526
838201LV00086B/5119